THE G.I. SERIES

Longknives:
The U.S. Cavalry and Other Mounted Forces, 1845–1942

Cover: A mounted dragoon major (indicated by orange trim and the 1851-pattern cap with pompon) meets a captain of cavalry. The period is 1855 to 1857, when there were five regiments of 'Longknives' in the U.S. Army: two of dragoons, two of cavalry, and one of mounted riflemen. In 1855 the two cavalry regiments were required to wear a black hat which looped up on the right side; it was the forerunner of the hat adopted for the entire Army in 1858. The cord, which was suspended from the front and back of the crown, is not indicated in this 19th century painting by H. A. Ogden. (AMWH)

The double-breasted coatee worn by Second Lieutenant Bezaleel Wells Armstrong of the Second Regiment of Dragoons was of dark blue wool with yellow facing material on the cuffs, collar, and turnbacks of the tails. Ornamental gold lace trimmed the collar; two gold lace borders surrounded the buttons on the cuffs of lieutenants, three for captains, and four for field grade officers. Gilt epaulettes topped the shoulders, with plain straps for second lieutenants, bars, oak leaves, or eagles being added to distinguish first lieutenants up to the regiment's colonel. The trousers were of light blue wool with double ½-inch yellow stripes of facing material. His sash was orange. Armstrong's head-dress is the 1839-pattern forage cap rather than the tall dress cap with gold suspension and breast cord called for by regulations. (LC)

THE G.I. SERIES

THE ILLUSTRATED HISTORY OF THE AMERICAN SOLDIER, HIS UNIFORM AND HIS EQUIPMENT

Longknives

The U.S. Cavalry and Other Mounted Forces, 1845–1942

Kurt Hamilton Cox and John P. Langellier

Greenhill Books
LONDON

Stackpole Books
PENNSYLVANIA

Greenhill Books

Longknives: The U.S. Cavalry and Other Mounted Forces, 1845–1942 first published 1996 by Greenhill Books, Lionel Leventhal Limited, Park House, 1 Russell Gardens, London NW11 9NN
and
Stackpole Books, 5067 Ritter Road, Mechanicsburg, PA 17055, USA.

British Library Cataloguing in Publication Data
Cox, Kurt Hamilton
Longknives: The U.S. Cavalry and Other Mounted Forces 1845–1942. – (G.I.: The Illustrated History of the American Soldier, His Uniform & His Equipment; Vol. 3)
1. Cavalry – United States – History
I. Title II. Series III. Langellier, John P.
357.1'0973
ISBN 1-85367-233-5

Library of Congress Cataloging-in-Publication Data available

Designed and edited by DAG Publications Ltd
Designed by David Gibbons.
Layout by Anthony A. Evans.
Printed and bound in Hong Kong.

ACKNOWLEDGEMENTS

In addition to the various institutions and individuals who have provided images for this publication the authors wish especially to thank Casey Barthelmess, John Carter, Gordon Chappell, Paula Chavoya, Susan Einstein, James Enos, Donald Kloster, Laurie Morrow, Harry Roach, Glen Swanson, Margaret Vining and Michael Winey. This book is dedicated to William R. Cox and his fellow troopers of the U.S. Cavalry.

ABBREVIATIONS

AHS	Arizona Historical Society
AMWH	Autry Museum of Western Heritage
CBFC	Christian Barthelmess Family Collection
FAM	Frontier Army Museum, Fort Leavenworth, KS
FDNHS	Fort Davis National Historic Site
FSHM	Fort Sam Houston Museum, Ripley Collection
JSM	Jeffrey S. Mosser Collection
KHC	Kurt Hamilton Cox
LBBNM	Little Bighorn Battlefield National Monument
LC	Library of Congress
NA	National Archives
RK	Robert Kotchian Collection
RBM	Reno Battlefield Museum
UK	University of Kansas Libraries, Kansas Collection, Pennell Collection
USAMHI	U.S. Army Military History Institute, Carlisle Barracks, PA
USCM	U.S. Cavalry Museum, Fort Riley, KS

LONGKNIVES:
THE U.S. CAVALRY AND OTHER MOUNTED FORCES, 1845–1942

From the American Revolution to the first quarter of the nineteenth century the story of the horse soldier in the U.S. Army was a chequered one. Time and again these mounted forces came into existence during periods of major conflict, but disappeared with the return of peace. This pattern continued until the U.S. government perceived a need for a permanent mounted arm, which was established in 1833 with the creation of the Regiment of Dragoons.

Within three years this unit was joined by another. With that the original outfit became the First Regiment of Dragoons while the newly established unit was designated the Second Regiment of Dragoons. By 1843, however, fiscal considerations caused the Second Dragoons to give up their horses, sabers, and carbines and be converted to a rifle regiment.

These actions provoked agitation in and out of the old Second for a return of status to dragoons, a movement which achieved success by 1844. Not long after that, the regiment was off to Texas to join Brigadier General Zachary Taylor as part of a military build-up taking place between the U.S.A. and Mexico. In 1845 the two countries went to war.

After three years of hard fighting against a formidable enemy, the Gringos ultimately prevailed. In many of the campaigns and battles between the neighboring nations, both the First and Second Dragoons participated as shock troops, escorts, and in other capacities, as did a short-lived Third Regiment of Dragoons and another organization, the Regiment of Mounted Rifles. This last named unit carried Model 1841 rifled muskets. Although they regularly rode into combat, theoretically they would dismount once in place and perform as foot soldiers. In truth, during most of the history of the American horse soldier fighting on foot formed at least as much a part of the mission as did mounted engagements.

Victory over Mexico also brought the United States vast new territory. Thereafter the dragoons and mounted riflemen would be scattered from the Mississippi River to the Pacific Coast and from the Mexican border to the Canadian border, in small posts with one or two companies as garrisons.

One of the assignments which fell to the dragoons and riflemen was the prevention of Indians in Mexico from entering the United States, and vice versa. The troopers also acted as a frontier constabulary in an effort to prevent hostilities between the Indians and ever increasing numbers of whites who came to the West. As the stream of settlers and adventurers increased, clashes with American Indians heightened.

Responding to these situations, the United States Congress deemed it necessary to add two more mounted regiments to the military establishment. In 1855 the First and Second Dragoons and the Regiment of Mounted Rifles (all formed prior to 1848) would be joined by the First and Second Cavalry regiments. The two units had scarcely assembled at their respective duty stations at Fort Leavenworth, Kansas Territory, and Jefferson Barracks, Missouri, when the First Cavalry were ordered to take the field. In the meantime troopers of the Second Cavalry went to Texas. For the remainder of the decade the latter unit engaged in numerous skirmishes with the Comanche, Kiowa and other bands that roamed the Lone Star State. During the same period, the First Cavalry responded to yet another duty, the maintenance of order between abolitionist and pro-slavery factions who were fighting over Kansas' status pending its admission to the Union. Would it be a free state or another bastion for slave holders?

When not occupied in the growing sectarian conflict, the First Cavalry responded to the Cheyenne and their increased unrest, as the tide of westward expansion rose. For instance, in 1856 Captain G. H. Stewart led a company and a half of troopers on a punitive expedition against a war party which had struck the Salt Lake City mail coach. Locating the raiders, Stewart attacked their village, killing ten warriors and wounding a like number. The stunned Cheyenne soon rallied and vigorously pursued Stewart on his return march.

During the following summer the First Cavalry's commander, Colonel E. V. Sumner (nicknamed 'Old Bull'), determined to quell the Cheyennes' unrest. On 29 July 1857, along the banks of the Solomon River, he found 'a large body' of the enemy 'drawn up in battle array, with their left resting upon the stream and their right covered by a bluff'. Facing an estimated 300 warriors, the colonel brought his six companies, 'into a line, and, without halting, detached the two flank companies at a gallop to turn their flanks'. Standing their ground, the resolute Cheyenne awaited the bluecoats' onslaught. Instead of charging with pistol or carbine, 'Old Bull' called for sabers to be drawn and brought to 'tierce point'. Galloping forward, the gleaming blades of the riders eventually sent the Indians in all directions. Sumner's bravado won the day. He lost two killed and eleven wounded, including Lieutenant J. E. B. Stuart. The villagers fled, leaving behind 171 lodges and considerable belongings which Sumner ordered to be destroyed.

In the same month, Lieutenant J. B. Hood led his company of the Second Cavalry on an equally dramatic foray in Texas. Spotting a band of American Indians at a distance, Hood proceeded cautiously. He moved ahead to parley, halting nearly thirty yards away from five warriors who carried a flag. At this point the Indians dropped their sign of truce and set fire to rubbish which they had collected to provide a smoke-screen. Then thirty warriors rose from behind Spanish bayonet plants within ten paces of the troopers and opened up with arrows and firearms. The patrol let out a yell and charged, and a hand-to-hand mêlée ensued. Outnumbered two to one, the pony soldiers were obliged to withdraw, but covered their orderly retreat with Colt revolvers. A half dozen of their number had been killed or wounded; Hood, among the latter, went on to become a Confederate general. This was one of at least forty fire fights in which the Second were engaged while in Texas, and hostilities increased to the extent that five companies of the First Cavalry joined the Second during an 1859 campaign against Indians and Mexican raiders along the Rio Grande. But the duel between the 'Longknives', as the cavalrymen were called by some Indian groups because of their sabers, and the original inhabitants of the West was not the only concern of the horse soldiers. Sectional differences increasingly contributed to lawlessness in Kansas that virtually became a rehearsal for the civil war.

Ultimately the tensions increased between the North and South. In April 1861 the long awaited storm broke with the bombardment of Fort Sumter, the federal stronghold in Charleston Harbor. President Abraham Lincoln responded with a call to arms, soliciting 75,000 volunteers for three months' duty. It soon became evident that this brief period of enlistment and the numbers of men demanded in the face of Southern secession would be inadequate for the task ahead.

Lincoln's next levy of troops included more volunteers and the expansion of the regulars by, among others, another regiment of cavalry, the Third, in 1861, which unlike the other mounted units consisted of twelve rather than ten companies. Not long after the Third came into being, its designation was changed as were those of all the regular mounted units, the dragoons becoming the First and Second Cavalry respectively, and the Mounted Rifles the

Third Cavalry. The old First and Second Cavalry switched to the Fourth and Fifth Cavalry Regiments, and the newly established Third Cavalry was retitled the Sixth Cavalry.

During the course of the war, the six regular mounted regiments were dispersed to many theaters of operation. They would be joined by some 272 regiments of volunteers, as well as 45 separate battalions, and 78 separate companies, also of volunteers. Some commanders used these troopers as guards for supply trains, flankers, advance elements, and reconnaissance, but others, such as Philip H. Sheridan, wanted his mounted arm to function independently, and be used *en masse* against Confederate cavalry or infantry, as the situation dictated. Sheridan's raid on Richmond represented a classic example of this line of thinking.

In their deployment against the Confederate capital and in other engagements, the cavalry participated to varying degrees and their leaders achieved notable results in the process. Once the fighting ceased the nation again turned its eyes to the West, where the migration that had begun in the 1840s flowed on in ever larger waves. As had happened before the war, American Indians attempted to block this invasion.

Again Congress replied with an increase in the regular army, adding four more cavalry regiments in 1866: the Seventh, Eight, Ninth, and Tenth. The last two were distinct from previous cavalry units in that the rank and file were African Americans, many of whom had been enslaved.

During a quarter of a century of continuous assignments on the Great Plains, in Western mountains, and south-western deserts, the troopers of the Ninth and Tenth Cavalry regiments became seasoned veterans. Beginning in 1867, when these horse soldiers were little more than raw recruits, the Ninth Cavalry set out on the first of many campaigns against American Indians in the south-west.

For instance, during October 1867, two men of the Ninth were killed escorting mail near Howard Wells, Texas. Not long after, another man became a casualty at Eagle Springs. Immediately after Christmas of that year, Company 'K' endured a two-day attack by a large war party whom they finally drove off, but not before losing three more troopers. In January 1868, Company 'F' sustained sixteen assaults by a sizeable band of Indians. And so it continued during the eight years in which the Ninth attempted to bring peace to the Lone Star State. In the years which followed the Ninth gained more field experience, culminating in the fight with the Lakotas at Drexel Mission, South Dakota, an action fought the day after the tragic encounter at Wounded Knee, in 1890–1.

Over the decades, the Tenth experienced many similar actions, beginning with the Southern Cheyennes and other Plains Indians in the hard-fought Cheyenne War of 1867–9. Repeatedly, elements of the regiment crossed trails with brave foes. Initially contact with the tribes was infrequent, but by the summer of 1867 clashes between the Tenth and Indians in Kansas occurred with considerable regularity.

Until 1869, when the Tenth transferred to Indian Territory, clashes with Indians continued along the Union Pacific Railroad on a regular basis. Events of the next decade continued to keep elements of the regiment in the saddle. Troopers of the Tenth, as was the case with the Ninth, developed into campaigners with few equals, official reports of the 1870s to late 1880s being replete with many exciting episodes of bravado. Because of such exploits, the black troops acquired the nickname, 'buffalo soldier,' a term of respect which was bestowed upon them by some of the first Indians they came into contact with during the 1860s in Texas.

The other eight cavalry regiments in the West likewise saw their share of campaigning and other assignments, the Seventh Cavalry attaining particular note in the newspapers of the period, in the main because of its flamboyant lieutenant colonel, George Custer. Between 1866 and 1876 Custer and the Seventh took the field in Kansas, Indian Territory, and eventually found itself posted to the Northern Great Plains. It was on a hot Sunday in June 1876 that Custer and his immediate battalion rode into the pages of history at a place called Little Bighorn. The annihilation of Custer's immediate command constituted one of the worst defeats ever inflicted on a U.S. Army unit in its thousands of actions against the American Indians. This débâcle in part contributed to an expansion of the number of enlisted men in cavalry companies which were increased to a maximum of one hundred troopers throughout 1890 (the number had been less than ninety in the past), although many units were well under this authorization for most of the period.

Despite the victory of the Lakota, Cheyenne, and others in that encounter, the American Indian was fighting a valiant last ditch defense against an overwhelming force. By the 1890s the clash between Indians and non-Indians had all but ceased on the field of battle.

The cavalry, together with much of the military, now came under review. What was the proper mission for the army? There were multiple answers. Some cavalry units served as stewards of the national parks which began to come into being in the later part of the nineteenth century. Others policed the borders to the north and south or were called out when labor unrest threatened private property.

During this period of transition, several companies of cavalry were disbanded within each regiment as a scaling down of military strength. Some of these disbanded troops, as companies came to be called officially in 1883, although the term had been applied informally for some time prior to that pronouncement, were reconstituted. Troopers were to be enlisted from among Crow, Sioux, and other American Indian nations. This short-lived experiment in essence was an outgrowth of the use of Indian scouts who had been authorized in 1866. The concept was to turn these former warriors not only into disciplined soldiers, but also to assimilate them into white culture.

Within only a few years these all-Indian units had been phased out. The appearance of the Indian troopers coincided with many other initiatives that began to change the U.S. Cavalry in the late 1800s. Among other things, a new manual, based on the work of Major General Emory Upton and originally designed for infantry, began to replace the former tactics adopted decades earlier under Secretary of War Joel Poinsett. Starting in the early 1870s, for two decades Upton's drill remained the 'Bible' for foot and horse soldiers alike, the basic structure resting upon a movement of a set of fours. Beginning in 1891, however, distinct manuals were adopted for artillery, infantry, and cavalry, with the last mentioned arm operating from a squadron level consisting of two to four troops, each troop being divided into two, three, or four platoons, depending on how many sets of fours were available.

Because it had been rare for more than a few troops to operate together in the field, some military leaders conceived of the establishment of schools that would allow training of larger bodies of soldiers. This was the reason why the School of Application for Infantry and Cavalry came into being at Fort Leavenworth, Kansas, in 1881, followed half a dozen years later by the Cavalry and Light Artillery School at nearby Fort Riley, an institution which underwent many name changes until being disbanded in the mid-twentieth century.

Although certain efforts had been made in the years after the Civil War to prepare the cavalry for more conventional deployment against a foreign enemy, that arm, as was true of the rest of the army, was in a less than perfect position to respond to its next assignment. In 1898 the United States declared war on Spain. This prompted all the cavalry companies to be called in from the many posts where they were serving. Most came from garrisons in the West and gathered either in San Francisco for duty in the Philippines, or went via Chickamauga, Georgia, bound for Tampa, Florida, before shipping off to various points in the West Indies.

As the troopers mobilized, Congress enacted legislation on 26 April 1898 which re-activated the two troops per regiment that previously had been victims of a reduction in military strength. This same law added a lieutenant, a sergeant, four corporals, and 34 privates to a troop, thereby raising the strength of each to 104, and bringing a regiment to a maximum 1,262 officers and men, a considerably greater number than prior strength on paper or in reality. Moreover, three U.S. Volunteer cavalry regiments were raised, the First United States Cavalry Regiment gaining the most fame as the 'Rough Riders'. Colonel Leonard Wood commanded, but his lieutenant colonel, Theodore Roosevelt, went on from this service eventually to become president of the United States. He and his fellow Rough Riders remained in uniform for only a matter of months, but during that time served dismounted from late June to early August in Cuba where they formed part of the cavalry division sent under a former Confederate officer, now commissioned a major general of Volunteers, 'Fighting Joe' Wheeler. Wheeler's division also included the First, Third, Sixth, Ninth and Tenth Cavalry, all of whom left behind their sabers and horses, to be deployed on foot, with the exception of one squadron of the Second Cavalry. Obtaining horses in Cuba, Troops 'A', 'C', 'D', and 'F' of the Second provided an independent brigade and were assigned cavalry responsibilities, including escort duty for field artillery going to the front, courier service, and even functioning as litter-bearers for wounded comrades in some instances. While the independent brigade performed its duties on horseback, Wheeler's dismounted cavalry fought well at La Guasima on 24 June, and about a week later assaulted San Juan Hill, before pressing on to Santiago.

The war in Cuba soon ended, but by 1899 regular cavalry regiments were again called upon, in this case to deploy to another former Spanish possession, the Philippines. Several regiments were engaged there to suppress a committed Filipino independence movement and to occupy the islands once Spain had abandoned the country.

U.S. cavalrymen likewise found themselves in another foreign land, when in 1900 they were dispatched to far off China as part of a relief column sent to raise the siege at Peking during the Boxer Rebellion. With such growing overseas military commitments coupled with domestic duties, Congress added five more cavalry regiments to the U.S. Army in 1901, numbering them the Eleventh to the Fifteenth. As part of this expansion, another captain, three second lieutenants, a commissary sergeant, and two color sergeants were added to each of the new as well as older regiments' table of organization, and the enlisted strength of each went from 100 men to 164 per troop.

Thereafter the composition of the cavalry regiments and the army as a whole fluctuated, but throughout the first decade and a half of the twentieth century the cavalry regularly made up about one-fifth of the total force, about half of which was stationed along the United States–Mexican border by 1915. Many of these units participated in the so-called Punitive Expedition under John J. Pershing, some even riding into Mexico after Pancho Villa's raid on Columbus, New Mexico on 8 March 1916.

Fighting between Mexican revolutionaries and American troops ended relatively quickly. Pershing was soon promoted and then assigned as commander of the Allied Expeditionary Force, when the United States entered the Great War in 1917.

The cavalry was now organized in two divisions consisting of a headquarters, three brigades of three cavalry regiments each, a field artillery regiment, and other support units including engineers, signal corps, and an aero squadron. Those cavalry regiments not assigned to one of the two divisions were to form elements of seven infantry divisions. On mobilization, eight more cavalry regiments (Eighteenth–Twenty-fifth) were formed, but were soon converted to field artillery, trench warfare and the machine-gun having diluted the cavalry's traditional role. But the Second, Third, Sixth, and Fifteenth Cavalry Regiments did join the AEF in France, although their chief function was that of a remount service.

The Armistice of 1918 brought most of these troopers back across the Atlantic, where for more than two decades the cavalry faced increasing change as mechanization began to challenge the military value of the horse. Experiments combining mounts and vehicles took place during this transitional period, but by the eve of the Second World War the day of the horse soldier was virtually ended.

The last mounted action of the U.S. Army took place not long after Pearl Harbor when the Philippine Scouts of the Twenty-Sixth Regiment fought against the Japanese, before being forced to destroy their horses and withdraw on foot. With the elimination of the office of chief of cavalry in March 1942, mounted forces began to be converted to armored units or to other types of forces, although horses and mules were used for a short while with 'Merrill's Marauders' in India and Burma, and the Third Infantry Division deployed a mounted reconnaissance troop in Italy in 1943. From 1946 to 1952, mounted troops enjoyed a brief revival when a number of horse platoons served in the U.S. Constabulary in Europe, but with the disbandment of the Constabulary the era of the American horse soldier passed into history.

FOR FURTHER READING

Brackett, Albert G. *History of the United States Cavalry, From Formation of the Federal Government to the 1st of June 1863.* New York: Harper & Bros., 1865.

Herr, John K., and Wallace, Edward S. *The Story of the U.S. Cavalry.* New York: Bonanza Books, 1953.

Katcher, Philip. *U.S. Cavalry on the Plains 1850-90.* London: Osprey Publishing, 1985.

Langellier, John P. *U.S. Dragoons 1833-55.* London: Osprey Publishing, 1995.

Stubbs, Mary Lee, and Connor, Stanley Russell. *Armor-Cavalry Part I: Regular Army and Army Reserve.* Washington, DC: Office of the Chief of Military History, 1960.

Urwin, Gregory J. W. *The United States Cavalry: An Illustrated History.* London: Blandford, 1983.

Right: From 1833 until the end of 1851 dragoon officers (with the exception of colonels who in 1847 wore authorised *chapeaux de bras*) were required to wear a tall cap with gold breast cord and cap lines, and a white horsehair plume for second lieutenants, lieutenants and captains. Gold epaulets indicated rank and were worn on a coatee of fine quality dark blue wool faced in light yellow. Trousers were of sky-blue wool with reinforced seat and inner legs and bore double yellow stripes on the outer seams. The sash was to be orange, but Second Lieutenant James Clyman, whose uniform this was, procured a yellow sash when he obtained this outfit in 1833. (State of California Parks and Recreation Department)

Left: The 1833-pattern dress uniform for dragoon officers also included aiguillettes of twisted gold and silver cord worn on the right shoulder for field grade officers (majors and colonels) and officers of the regimental staff, as seen here in the case of Captain Thomas Swords, quartermaster of the First Dragoons. Three gold lace loops surrounding gilt dragoon buttons on yellow facing also appeared on the cuffs of coatees worn by captains; field grade officers had four of these ornamental trim elements, and lieutenants two. (WPM)

Below: Receiving orders before going into the Battle of Resaca during the Mexican War, men of the Second U.S. Dragoons appear in the 1833–51-pattern mounted jacket with yellow trim, and the yellow hat bands on their 1839-pattern forage caps which the Second Dragoons adopted in the mid-1840s to distinguish themselves from their comrades in the First Dragoons.

Left: In 1851 the trim for dragoons was to be orange rather than yellow, a change which coincided with a new series of uniform regulations calling for a single-breasted nine-button frock coat with orange facings on collars and cuffs; a plastron would cover the chest of bandsmen and buglers. Company grade officers wore a similar frock but without the facings. A cap topped by a pompon of orange was another distinctive feature. A similar uniform faced in emerald green was stipulated for mounted riflemen.

Left: According to General Orders No. 3, 24 March 1858, trousers were to be dark blue, and remained that shade until a return to sky-blue in 1861. So all the officers and men in this picture are wearing the uniform that was regulation for the years immediately preceding the Civil War. The mounted rifle officer on the left has a ⅛-inch emerald-green welt on his trousers, and the centers of his shoulder-straps are emerald-green; the dragoon major's welt is orange as are the centres of his shoulder-straps. Another indication that the man standing on the steps is a dragoon officer is the fact that he has a silver regimental numeral in the upper angle of his gold embroidered crossed sabers hat insignia, whereas cavalry officers had the same insignia but the numeral was below in accordance with General Orders No. 7, 24 June 1858. The dragoon sergeant at the far right is wearing the 1854-pattern enlisted jacket with orange facings. (AMWH)

Left: W. T. Trego captured a moment at the Battle of Gaines Mills, June 1862, with Union cavalrymen in their yellow worsted trimmed blue wool, cavalry 1855-pattern, uniform jackets, led by a first lieutenant in a four-button sack coat, the two most common outer garments for federal mounted regulars during the war. All are wearing forage caps, many of which bear the crossed sabers of cavalry, regimental numerals and company letters in brass. Although such insignia were not called for by general orders, the wearing of them was not uncommon. (USCM)

First Sergeant. 1872-5.

Sentinel. 1873-5.

Sound the Rally. 1875.

E FORBES.

Ready for Guard. 1875.

Scouting. 1873.

Left: Christian Barthelmess as drum major of the Sixth Cavalry from 1878 to 1879 offers one example of the variations possible for his position because bands could obtain special uniforms purchased through a regimental fund with the sanction of the regiment's commander. Consequently, Barthelmess's epaulets and aiguilettes are pre-1872 patterns while the triple-breasted dark blue wool coat never was an issue item although the gold lace on the sleeves is of the type worn by field grade officers from 1872 to 1880. The baldric, gold trim on the coat collar, and gold trimmed forage cap likewise are other deviations from the norm, but in keeping with the latitude for bandsmen. (CBFC)

Left: The top two figures and center figure depict the 1872-pattern enlisted cavalry dress uniform complete with plumed helmet. The coats of trumpeters and bandsmen were ornamented with herringbones (center mounted figure) while the breast of coats for all other enlisted personnel was plain dark blue wool. For garrison duty a blue forage cap and five-button blouse with yellow wool piping was regulation starting in 1874 (see lower left-hand corner), and a sky-blue woollen overcoat protected troopers from foul weather as seen in the right-hand corner. After 1879, capes were to be lined in the color of the branch, thus yellow for cavalry.

Right: A sergeant of the Ninth Cavalry, one of two U.S. cavalry regiments whose enlisted ranks were filled by African Americans beginning in 1866, appears in the dress uniform of 1884–5 which was the former 1872–6-pattern blouse with gold lace chevrons in lieu of the former pattern made of facing cloth. (SI)

Above: In 1880 gold lace was ordered to be removed from the sleeves of the officers' dress coat and the following year a new design of dress helmet replaced the earlier pattern of 1872. The officers' 1881-pattern usually was of cork and featured a buffalo or yak plume in yellow for cavalry. Light artillery officers and field grade officers of artillery were to wear the same helmet but with a slightly different eagle front plate and with a scarlet plume as seen here. (AMWH)

Above: In 1873 a new chevron was adopted for cavalry saddler sergeants, which featured a saddler's knife in yellow above three chevrons. The blouse on which it is worn is of the type which began to be used in 1884 when all trim was removed from five-button jackets for enlisted personnel save chevrons for NCOs. From 1872 until early in the 1900s, cavalry sergeants had 1-inch yellow leg stripes on their light blue woollen trousers, corporals ½-inch stripes. As of 1883 musicians and buglers had ½-inch stripes. The forage cap shown is of the 1872-pattern, the summer helmet on the infantry regimental quartermaster sergeant, with his white trim adopted in 1884, is of the 1880-pattern. The white stable uniform and the rust-brown fatigue uniform are also typical of the issue for cavalry enlisted personnel from the mid-1880s until the early twentieth century. (AMWH)

Right: A cavalry officer in the 1895-pattern concealed button blouse trimmed in mohair is wearing the 1889-pattern campaign hat and the yellow lined officer's cape. His boots are the M1889 worn over sky-blue kersey breeches, this latter item being adopted in 1898.

Left: The officer's dress helmet and knots of the 1887–1903 period, in this case worn by First Lieutenant B. Dorcy of the Fourth Cavalry. In 1887 the yellow of cavalry facings was changed to a darker shade. (AHS)

Right: Captain Nathan Boone wears the distinctive shoulder-straps prescribed for dragoon officers from 1839 to 1851 as indication of rank. These were of dark blue wool to match the frock coat, with a gold border and gilt crescents at the end. The rank insignia and regimental numeral appeared on these accessories. (SHSM)

Left: Colonel Stephen Watts Kearny, who commanded the First Dragoons from the early 1830s until the mid-1840s, sat for a portrait which provides a clear detail of the collar of the 1833-pattern officer's dress coatee. The lace was gold and the facings yellow. (NA)

Left: The collar of the 1833–51 dragoon officers' dress coatee of gold lace with yellow facing beneath is even more evident on the coat of Colonel Richard Mason, who commanded the First Regiment of Dragoons during the War with Mexico, replacing Kearny who was promoted to brigadier general. (NA)

Right: Lieutenant Colonel Charles May wears an untrimmed coatee, which was authorized for undress from 1833 to 1839, and the blue shoulder-straps with gold lace trim and crescent unique to dragoon officers from 1839 to 1851 (although adopted by some other officers unofficially), and a non-regulation sword belt in lieu of the black leather one prescribed during the period until the early 1850s. (LC)

Left: When the Regiment of Mounted Rifles was established, its officers and men wore the dragoon field uniform but with dark blue trousers rather than sky-blue, and the trouser stripes were black with a yellow border. Captain Benjamin Roberts, seen here in about 1847, served with the regiment during the Mexican War. He is wearing the waist-length dark blue woollen jacket with gold lace trim which, although not mentioned in orders or regulations, was applied to many officers' garments in a fashion similar to the worsted lace of the other ranks. He wears standard shoulder-straps rather than the special epaulette-like ones of dragoons, and the gilt buckle of his saber belt seems to bear a script 'R.' (USAMHI)

Above: The dress uniform prescribed for dragoon enlisted men in 1833 remained virtually unchanged until the early 1850s, the only difference being that initially NCOs' chevrons were worn points up, but as of 1847 points down, as seen in this sketch of a first sergeant at Fort Snelling, Minnesota, in 1851. (NA)

Above: A rare picture of a private of dragoons in the 1854-pattern uniform coat and the cap prescribed in the same year. All facings for dragoons were orange lace around the edges of the collar and cuffs, and orange piping between the upper and lower parts of the cap. Shoulder scales were of brass. This cap and coat remained regulation until 1858, although the latter garment continued in use for some years after. (SI)

Above right: A double-breasted dark blue woollen frock coat with seven gilt eagle buttons in each row indicated a field grade officer (majors and colonels) as is the case for David Hunter, the commanding colonel of the First Cavalry, as he appeared in about 1858. (USAMHI)

Opposite page: First Lieutenant Roger Jones of the Regiment of Mounted Rifles. Beside him is his 1858-pattern officer's hat with its distinctive perpendicular gold embroidered trumpet ornament. A silver numeral '1' appears in the loop of the trumpet, although there was no reason to designate the regiment with a numeral because it was the only regular army mounted rifle outfit in existence. Jones cradles an M1850 foot officer's sword, and his single-breasted dark blue woollen frock coat indicates that he is a company grade officer; his epaulettes further establish his rank and regiment. From 1858 until 1861 his trousers would have been dark blue with a ⅛-inch emerald-green welt (for mounted rifle officers) let into the outer seams. (USMHI)

Above: Captain Thomas Wood of the First Cavalry has retained the gold cords on his 1855-pattern hat, but has added the new gold embroidered crossed saber devices prescribed in 1858. Originally cavalry officers wore this insignia with edges downward as per General Orders No. 3, Adjutant General's Office, 24 March 1854. Woods wears his shoulder-straps over his epaulettes, a practice which essentially was abandoned in the late 1850s, the year this portrait was probably taken. (USAMHI)

Above: In this *circa* 1860 picture Lieutenant Bowman is wearing an enlisted sky-blue woollen mounted overcoat rather than the officer's dark blue woollen 'cloakcoat'. His cape is longer than the 1851-pattern issued. (USAMHI)

Right: Second Lieutenant Charles Bowman displays the numeral '1' in silver below his officer's hat insignia in keeping with the directive for cavalry officers to do so set forth in General Orders No. 7, Adjutant General's Office, 24 June 1858. (USAMHI)

Above: The enlisted forage cap of the late 1850s was to have a welt around the top in orange for dragoons, yellow for cavalry, and emerald-green for mounted riflemen, a practice which had been discontinued by 1861. Here, in about 1858, a dragoon stands to horse at Fort Leavenworth, Kansas, in the pre-1861 forage cap with the 1854-pattern mounted jacket trimmed in orange worsted lace. (LC)

Left: In 1854 lace trim replaced the plastron on the front of jackets for musicians and bandsmen, as seen here in this portrait of a cavalry bugler with the 1858–72 hat. Note that because yellow registered black on photographs of the time, the photographer has painted in the details of the lace, a common practice during this period when details might be lost or obscured. The trumpeter wears a sash, although this practice supposedly was restricted to the chief trumpeter of each regiment, and all NCOs from first sergeant up. (Scott Harmon Collection)

Right: A member of the California 100, men who came from California but served with the state of Massachusetts as part of the federal forces, wears a uniform that was almost identical with that of the regular army except for the brass insignia on the cap which reads 'CAL 100', and has sabers and company as well as regimental designations. The trousers are of sky-blue wool and reinforced to prolong wear on horseback. The boots are one of many types of privately purchased footgear of the Civil War era. (William Langlois Collection)

Above: Company 'K' of the First United States Cavalry was one of the few regular army mounted units to fight in the Civil War. They pose here in February 1864 at Brandy Station, Virginia, in a mix of uniforms from the 1854-pattern mounted jacket trimmed in yellow worsted tape for enlisted men, to the four-button sack coat. The three officers standing in the center front also exhibit several types of garments including: on the left, an officer who evidently has obtained an enlisted 1851-pattern sky-blue overcoat with its cape removed; the center officer (leaning on his saber) wears the company grade single-breasted nine-button officer's frock; the third officer wears an officer's version of the mounted jacket but with nine buttons down the front rather than twelve which was the regulation number for enlisted men. Either he has had a nine-button frock coat modified by removing the skirts, which some enlisted men did with the issue 1858-pattern frock, or his tailor simply used the basic design of the upper portion of the coat but turned it into a jacket. (LC)

Right: From 1851 to 1872 field grade officers were to have a double-breasted blue woollen frock coat with seven eagle buttons in each row. The breast of the eagle devices bore a 'C' on the shield for cavalry officers. Both shoulder-straps and epaulettes could be worn depending on the order of dress required. This major or lieutenant colonel is wearing shoulder-straps, and is holding a forage cap with embroidered crossed sabers in gold with a silver '4' to indicate his cavalry regiment. He wears a dark blue vest which was an option for officers. He has either turned down his collar, thereby exposing the black velvet lining, or has substituted a roll collar of black velvet for the more traditional stand-up collar. (FSHM)

Above: Joseph G. Everett wears the chevrons of a first sergeant, a position he held with Company 'M', Seventh Cavalry, Missouri Volunteers, during the Civil War. These insignia were of worsted yellow tape sewn to material that matched the mounted jacket. Sergeant Everett has turned down the collar of his jacket, a relatively common practice to prevent chafing and similar discomforts. (SHSM)

Above: Myles Walter Keogh appears in essentially the regulation uniform of 1866–72 for a company grade officer of the Seventh United States Cavalry of which he was a captain, except that he is wearing some of his medals from service in the Papal forces, a corps badge from his Civil War duty with the Union Army, and a non-regulation black campaign hat which he has modified to conform for the most part to the 1858-pattern regulation hat complete with two ostrich feathers for officers below the rank of major. (Elizabeth Lawrence Collection)

Left: In contrast to his fellow Seventh Cavalry captain, Albert Barnitz has a non-regulation piped shirt, custom boots, a broad slouch hat without insignia, and gauntlets, all part of his field kit which he has donned for this picture taken in early 1868. (Courtesy Robert M. Utley)

Below: Men of Troop 'I' of the Eighth Cavalry in New Mexico *circa* 1870 still wear the jacket and forage cap adopted a decade earlier. On the left the lace trim can be seen on the two company trumpeters, while the officer in the front of the unit is wearing his nine-button frock coat. (KSHS)

Right: In 1872, the officers' 1858-pattern hat gave way to a new helmet for the cavalry which bore the arms of the United States in gilt metal with a silver regimental numeral (in this case a '7' for Lieutenant B. Hodgson of the Seventh Cavalry) for officers. The plume was yellow horsehair. The dress coat adopted for company grade officers in the same year had gold lace ornaments on both cuffs, and cavalry officers' small buttons surmounted the lace at the points. The field grade officers' coat bore three such devices. (LBBNM)

Opposite page, left: A Fourth Cavalry company grade officer has dispensed with his helmet and substituted a non-regulation 'pillbox' cap. Otherwise he is attired strictly 'by the book' for the period 1872 to 1880. (NA)

Opposite page, right: Private George Walker of the Seventh Cavalry appears in the 1872-pattern enlisted dress cavalry uniform with its yellow collar, cuff, and tail flashes and trim around the outer edges of the blue woollen coat that was single-breasted and fastened with nine 1854-pattern enlisted buttons. The reinforcement is evident on the inner trouser legs. Walker died at the Little Bighorn. (RBM)

Above: Ninth Cavalry troopers at Fort Davis, Texas wear the 1872-pattern cavalry dress uniform, although it was some time before that unit received this dress garb to replace their former issue. Note the trumpeter on the far left of the image rides a gray or white horse to set him off from his fellow troopers on their darker mounts. (FDNHS)

Right: Private Gustave Korn of the Seventh Cavalry also appears in the 1872-pattern dress uniform as he attends one of the most famous military horses of the nineteenth century, Captain Keogh's mount Comanche, who survived the Little Bighorn battle of 1876. (LBBNM)

Left: Trumpeter Aloys Bohner appears in the 1872-pattern cavalry dress coat for musicians with yellow herringbones on the chest. The gauntlets are private purchase or a photographer's prop because these items were not issued to the rank and file until the 1880s. (RBM)

Above: From the late 1860s until the 1870s (when this photograph was taken) Lieutenant Colonel George Custer favored a hunting jacket of buckskin as seen here in this group of members of his regiment, officers from other units, and civilians. The officer to Custer's left has donned a bib-front shirt popular with firemen, frontiersmen, other non-military men of the period and some officers. He is also wearing the 1872-pattern folding hat, although sideways, perhaps as a comic gesture. (LBBNM)

Right: Sergeant E. D. Gibson of the Tenth Cavalry has taken the liberty of adding yellow piping all along the edges of his 1874 pattern enlisted blouse, although such cord trim was called for only around the collar and as cuff ornamentation. His blouse displays no chevrons, perhaps because prior to General Order No. 21, 20 March 1876, chevrons were mentioned only for wear on the dress jacket and overcoat. His trousers are of sky-blue kersey, and the reinforcement of the same color can be seen on the inner legs. The stripe is yellow and was to be 1-inch wide. Gibson holds an 1876-pattern campaign hat in his left hand. The vest, shirt, and tie are private purchase, not government issue. (FAM)

Top: A motley group of Sixth Cavalry troopers at Fort Grant, Arizona Territory, in 1883, showing a variety of issue and non-issue wear. Most are wearing the 1874-pattern enlisted blouse with its collar and cuffs piped in yellow except the man on the far right in the rear row who has retained the 1872-pattern nine-button pleated blouse with the yoke, collar, and cuffs piped in yellow. The soldier at the far left has unhooked his 1872-pattern folding hat which he has adorned with a yellow hat cord and 1872-pattern cavalry brass sabers, not commonly used on head-dress as indicated by the absence of such insignia on all the other hats seen here. The man seated on the left has an oil cloth cover on his 1872-pattern forage cap, and the three men to his left appear to be wearing the 1876-pattern campaign hat; everyone else has adopted civilian head-dress. Finally,

an 1881-pattern piped blue shirt is just visible on the man seated second from right, so indicated by the yellow piping which trims the front. (AHS)

Above: Another group of Sixth Cavalry troops, this time from Company 'B' at San Carlos, Arizona Territory, appear in field uniforms which are anything but uniform. Many of the men appear to be wearing the new 1883-pattern drab campaign hat which was popular with soldiers. Most seem to have 1872-pattern boots, and some of them are wearing the 1883-pattern shirt. Only one of the group (sixth from the left) is wearing a private purchase bandanna, an accessory which was not evident in most photographs of the era, Hollywood notwithstanding. (Los Angeles County Museum of Natural History)

Below: Apache scouts join troopers of either the Sixth or Fourth Cavalry in Arizona in about 1886. Both soldiers are wearing 1884-pattern boots and neckerchiefs. The man on the left carries an infantry rifle and a revolver in what seems to be an M1881 holster, the man on the right has a .45-70 caliber Springfield carbine, the regular issue longarm for cavalry. The same soldier and one of the scouts seem to be wearing fringed gauntlets rather than the regulation issue 1884-pattern. (AHS)

Bottom: A large group of Indian scouts under the command of Captain Emmet Crawford, Sixth Cavalry (standing in

doorway, large hat with turned-up brim), gather at Fort Grant, Arizona Territory, in 1886. Many of them are wearing a combination of military uniform components, civilian garb, and traditional Apache dress; the officers with them likewise are wearing a composite of military and frontier civilian styles. The man standing near the corner of the adobe building wears an 1880-pattern summer helmet, the officer to his left has more of a regulation appearance with his 1875-pattern five-button officers' blouse, 1884-pattern gauntlets, and probably an 1883-pattern drab campaign hat. (AHS)

cowboys of the period. They are wearing the 1883-pattern blue shirt with the exception of the man next to the burro who has the type of five-button enlisted blouse without piping which came into use in 1883. Several of the hats have broad brims, which makes it likely that their wearers have replaced their issue 1883-pattern campaign hat by civilian versions. (FDNHS)

Opposite page, top: Tenth Cavalry and Eighth Infantry officers with Apache scouts, photographed in about 1886. Despite the Arizona climate, they look crisp in their 1875-pattern officers' blouses with shoulder-straps to indicate rank (yellow centers for cavalry and white for infantry) and 1883-pattern campaign hats. Most have Mills woven cartridge belts. The man holding a rifle instead of a carbine has an M1880 hunting knife on his belt. (AHS)

Opposite page, bottom: In 1886 Captain Henry Lawton and men of the Fourth Cavalry are on hand to transport Apache prisoners to Florida after the conclusion of the so-called Geronimo campaigns. Lawton and most of the men are wearing the 1883-pattern drab campaign hat and five-button blouses. Chevrons of yellow facing material are evident on the sleeves of several NCOs, as are the shoulder-straps of the three officers. Some of the men are wearing 1883-pattern blue shirts. (AHS)

Above: In nearby New Mexico Territory an unidentified trooper stands to horse with his carbine in a leather boot, adopted in 1885, suspended from an unusually modified M1874 McClellan saddle. He has acquired a civilian butt-backward holster as a practical replacement for the butt-forward military holster with flap, and has

hung his saber from the Mills canvas cartridge belt, despite the fact that this weapon was of little use in the field against Indians. (NA)

Below: In about 1886, some individuals from Troop 'G' Sixth Cavalry, in New Mexico Territory, have obtained holsters commonly associated with

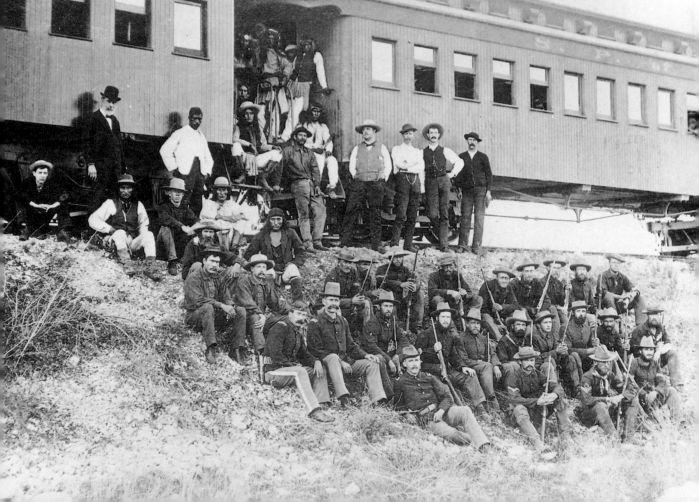

Opposite page, top: Sergeant John Bouck (left) and Corporal Sampson at Fort Custer, Montana Territory, in 1886, wearing the regulation issue for that period. The sergeant has a holster made two decades earlier, the issue of old-pattern accouterments and uniforms being not uncommon. Note that Sampson has an M1880 hunting knife on his belt. His ½-inch leg stripes are those of a corporal, Bouck's the 1-inch for sergeants, both of yellow facing material. Both men are wearing the M1884 boots and the 1884-pattern gauntlets which saw fairly widespread distribution soon after being introduced. By the mid-1880s the campaign outfit had become more uniform than it had been in the previous decade. (NA)

Left: Troop 'C' Third Cavalry NCOs and privates decided that their sabers would add a fine touch to this 1886–7 posed photograph taken among the rocks near their garrison. Many of the men have added various types of neckerchiefs to spruce up their field kit, although these privately purchased items could serve practical purposes. A few have chosen to wear civilian shirts rather than the 1883-pattern blue issue shirt which most are wearing. Some of the men have 1885-pattern marksmanship buttons on the collars of their five-button blouse, and almost all have 1884-pattern trousers, boots, and gauntlets, demonstrating the degree of uniformity achieved by this time. An exception is the peculiar way in which many of the men have blocked their 1883-pattern campaign hats, unlike the regulation fore and aft crease. (FDNHS)

Above: Seventh Cavalry officers at Wounded Knee, South Dakota, in 1890, wearing the 1889-pattern campaign hat or the 1872-pattern forage cap. With the exception of the surgeon, who is wearing the 1885-pattern officers' dark blue ulster overcoat, these officers are wearing the 1875-pattern five-button blouse with shoulder-straps. Yellow 1½-inch leg stripes can be seen on many of the light blue trousers. (USCM)

Above: Three companies of the First Cavalry at Fort Grant, Arizona Territory appear in the 1872-pattern forage cap associated with garrison wear along with webbed cartridge belts that were usually part of the field kit. The guidons are of the 1885-pattern, and the photo of this mounted inspection dates from *circa* 1890. (NA)

Below: Besides military applications horses were used for pleasure purposes, such as in this case where cavalry officers and their ladies at Fort Riley, Kansas prepare to ride with their hounds on a hunt in the late 1880s. (USCM)

Opposite page: A corporal of the Ninth Cavalry at Pine Ridge Agency, South Dakota, during the Ghost Dance, has slid his holster around to the left side to display his .45 caliber Colt revolver. The blanket on his pommel is non-regulation and may have been obtained at the Indian agency during the cold winter of 1890/1. His hat seems to have a larger brim than the issue item, and is possibly also a private purchase. He has attached a breast collar to his McClellan saddle which, again, is atypical for the period. (NSHS)

Above: The slight flair or 'springbottom' to the cuffs of these soldiers' trousers was adopted in the 1870s as a concession to fashion. In this *circa* 1885 picture of troopers and horses being trained to stay still under fire, the officers have 1½-inch yellow leg stripes. The private in the center has no trouser stripes in keeping with regulations which prescribed this trim for NCOs and commissioned officers only. (NA)

Left: The first African American graduate of West Point, Henry O. Flipper, is seen here with an 1875-pattern officer's five-button blouse. The black mohair binding on the collar and along the outer seam was optional, but was often worn. Plain shoulder-straps with a yellow center indicate Flipper's rank as a second lieutenant of the Tenth Cavalry. (AMWH)

Right: Another second lieutenant, in this case of the Seventh Cavalry, is wearing the 1872-officers' pattern forage cap with gold embroidered crossed sabers device surmounted by a silver embroidered '7'. The gold cord cap strap is of the pattern sanctioned by General Order No. 102, 26 December 1883, prior to which many officers had worn it unofficially rather than the stipulated leather strap. This officer has also chosen to have mohair trim on his blouse.

Above: Marksmanship devices came into use from the late 1870s. This unidentified cavalry sergeant has affixed a pair of 1885-pattern marksmanship buttons to the collar of his post-1884 five-button blouse. The white linen dress collar beneath the blouse is of the type adopted at the end of 1886 to help prevent soiling of the uniform coat or blouse from perspiration. (FAM)

Above right: In addition to the marksmanship buttons for collars, a cross suspended from a bar was authorized for sharpshooters as of 1885, to be worn on the left breast, as seen on this sergeant of Troop 'F' Second Cavalry. He

appears in the typical enlisted men's garrison wear of the 1885–5 period. (UK)

Opposite page: Captain Henry Ripley of the Third Cavalry holds the 1881-pattern officers' dress helmet and wears custom gauntlets as well as aiguillettes which were restricted to regimental adjutants and aides. The plume is dark yellow as are the backings to his shoulder knots. In addition to his sharpshooter medal, Ripley displays medals from veterans' organizations. His belt is of gold lace with three horizontal yellow stripes in keeping with regulation for company grade cavalry officers. (FSHM)

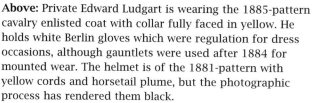

Above: Private Edward Ludgart is wearing the 1885-pattern cavalry enlisted coat with collar fully faced in yellow. He holds white Berlin gloves which were regulation for dress occasions, although gauntlets were used after 1884 for mounted wear. The helmet is of the 1881-pattern with yellow cords and horsetail plume, but the photographic process has rendered them black.

Above right: Herringbones continued to ornament the front of the bugler's dress coat, as seen here on a trumpeter wearing an 1885-pattern cavalry dress coat. The herringbones were yellow worsted to match the facings of the coat. (Jerome Green Collection)

Opposite page, top: With sabers drawn buffalo soldiers from the Tenth Cavalry practice with this obsolete edged weapon in a mock charge. The image was taken around 1892 at Fort Keogh, Montana. (CBFC)

Opposite page, center: Responding to officers' call at a parade formation, cavalry officers appear in the 1881-pattern dress helmet at Fort Riley, Kansas while their troops appear in formation in the background. (USCM)

Opposite page, bottom: Two troops of the Tenth Cavalry depict the typical practice of assigning horses according to color to each company within a regiment, except Troop M that usually received mixed colors. These men appear in the field kit commonly seen in the late 1880s through the late 1890s. (NA)

Above: This side view of a trumpeter shows the double ½-inch yellow leg stripes which were authorized in 1883 but often worn without official sanction prior to that date. He is wearing the 1885-pattern coat and 1881-pattern helmet. This uniform remained regulation until 1903. (NA)

Opposite page: This Second Cavalry bandsman at Fort Wingate, New Mexico Territory, has put aside his helmet for a busby. Other alterations to the regulation uniform include the lyre belt buckle, the trefoil on his cuffs, and the triple row of buttons. Worsted aiguillettes with shoulder knots in yellow to match the facings of the coat and trouser stripes were adopted in the mid-1880s for bandsmen. (USAMHI)

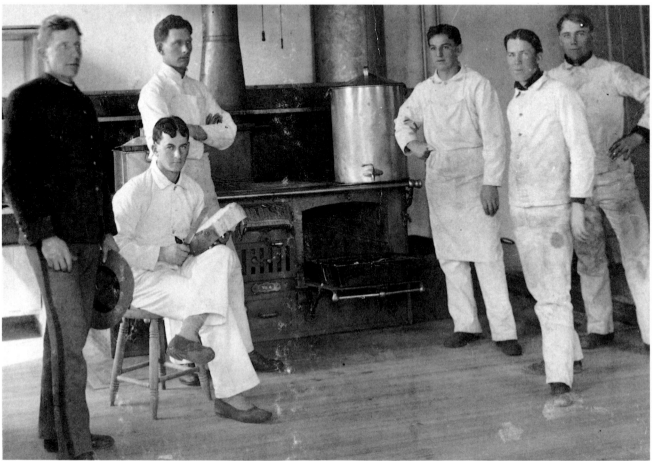

Opposite page, top: In this *circa* 1891 picture, cavalrymen at Fort Huachuca, Arizona Territory, march out to tend their horses. They are wearing the light canvas or unbleached drill three-button stable coat with stand-up collar, and matching trousers, both of the 1879-pattern, although similar coats had been provided for several decades prior to this date. They are also wearing the drab 1889-pattern campaign hat. (AMWH)

Opposite page, bottom: Another use for a white work outfit is evident in this kitchen scene of men from Troop 'C', Fourth Cavalry, at Fort Riley, Kansas, *circa* 1890, in that most of the men appear in the 1888- or 1889-pattern five-button summer sack coat of cotton duck. This jacket could be worn with regulation 1884-pattern buttons or with white vegetable ivory buttons, both options being secured by toggles or split rings. The sergeant on the left wears the

standard dark blue post-1884 woollen blouse and sky-blue kersey trousers with 1-inch yellow leg stripe.

Above left: In 1895 a new pattern forage cap with sloping visor was adopted for officers and other ranks alike. This private of Troop 'E', Fifth Cavalry, is wearing the new cap with its one-piece brass insignia which was attached by means of a screw post and nut. The trooper has chosen to wear his white duck trousers with his blue woollen blouse. (FSHM)

Above: The officers' version of the 1895-pattern forage cap bore the Arms of the United States on the front and had a black mohair band around the base as seen here on this second lieutenant of cavalry, who has also obtained the 1895-pattern officers' concealed-button blouse with black mohair trim. Gilt insignia appears on the collar. (UK)

Top: Troop 'C', First Cavalry, at Fort Riley, Kansas, wearing their 1895-pattern enlisted forage caps and the sky-blue kersey overcoat of the type adopted in the 1880s and which continued in use through the turn of the century, with minor modifications. The troopers have removed the detachable capes lined in yellow for this group photograph taken in about 1895. (USCM)

Above: The enlisted kersey overcoat with cape attached and folded back to reveal the yellow lining is evident in this picture of a cavalryman of Troop 'F', Eighth Cavalry, standing by a caparisoned horse in preparation for a funeral, with the 1884- or 1887-pattern boots in the reversed stirrups as a symbol of the deceased rider.

Below: Some members of Troop 'H', Second Cavalry, watch as their comrades clean M1885 McClellan saddles and the M1874 bridle with M1892 bit. The collar-less white shirt is a civilian item, but the dark undershirt of one of the two troopers standing in the center of the photograph appears to be of the issue type. One man has pressed a coat strap from a saddle into service as a belt to hold up his white duck trousers. (UK)

Left: Appearing in an 1884-pattern brown canvas sack coat with matching trousers, this mounted man was probably a member of the First Volunteer Cavalry, the unit which gained fame as 'The Rough Riders'. Before receiving regular uniforms and shipping to Cuba, some of the Rough Riders pressed these duck fatigue outfits into service. (FSHM)

Lower left: Troop 'L' of the Ninth Cavalry fielded a baseball team at Fort Wingate, NM, evidently pressing their 1883-pattern shirts into service as their outer garments with the application of their team 'name'. Two of their officers appear in the 1895-pattern blouse; one is wearing an 1889-pattern campaign hat, the other an 1895-pattern forage cap. The two enlisted men on the far right in the front row are wearing the 1899-pattern khaki blouse with detachable yellow shoulder-straps, and featuring a 'rolling' collar. The man at the extreme right seems to be wearing white duck trousers, and the corporal to his left is wearing sky-blue kersey, an unusual combination of uniform components. (Photograph by Imperial Photo Gallery, Courtesy Museum of New Mexico)

Above: 'Buffalo soldiers' (nickname for African American cavalrymen) in Cuba retained the types of uniform which had been issued to them from the 1880s until the late 1890s, despite the fact that the heavy wool was ill suited to the climate of that country. Several of the men are wearing the issue suspenders first specified in 1883 and modified slightly in 1887. Prior to the Spanish-American War these braces were seldom seen on the outside, being usually worn beneath the blouse. (USAMHI)

Right: In the 1880s leggings gradually began to replace high top boots for cavalrymen in the field as seen on this member of Troop 'B', Fourteenth Cavalry, who has a full-length scabbard for his Krag-Jorgensen carbine. Letters and numerals in brass to indicate troop and regiment can be seen, along with the yellow hat cord with acorn tips, both adopted in 1899. (UK)

Left: The hat cord and brass unit insignia likewise are evident in this picture of three men from Troop 'D', Fourteenth Cavalry, all of whom are wearing what appear to be 1896-pattern gauntlets, Mills belts with double rows of cartridges for the .30-40 caliber Krag, and sabers with black leather M1885 saber knots. (UK)

Right: Troop 'F', First Cavalry, at Fort Riley, Kansas, in 1897, wearing a variety of issue and non-issue items. In the former category the 1880-pattern summer helmet is of particular note, being held by the corporal on the left, nearest to the camera, the interior details being evident including the ventilator top and the adjustable sweatband. Three more men towards the rear are wearing the same pattern helmet which was made of cork covered with bleached or unbleached cotton drilling and with an emerald-green merino or cashmere lining on the interior of the visor. (UK)

Right: The Krag-Jorgensen carbine with a side-mounted magazine was adopted from 1896 for cavalrymen. The saddle blanket is the gray model with yellow woven stripe which was adopted in 1876. (UK)

Left: This Fourth Cavalry trooper in the Philippine Islands has reversed his .38 caliber Colt double-action revolver, which replaced the .45 caliber single-action from the 1890s, so that the weapon is more evident in this photograph.

Below: A troop of the Seventh Cavalry stand on horseback, while two officers in the 1898-pattern blue woollen field blouse with exterior pockets remain mounted. Khaki trousers with belt loops are evident on the enlisted men, these too being adopted in 1898.

Above: Standing in front of the 1886-pattern cavalry standard and national colors (that were authorized for cavalry in 1887), Color Sergeant Alexander of the Seventh Cavalry appears in the 1895-pattern forage cap and a pair of custom-made color sergeants' chevrons with a starburst rather than the five-pointed star specified in 1901, one year before this photograph was taken. (UK)

Below: Among other features of Troop 'E', Seventh Cavalry's group portrait are the screen vents on the 1899-pattern drab campaign hat which were re-introduced after similar devices were discontinued in lieu of perforations on the 1889-pattern campaign hat. The guidon with red upper and white lower sections is of the pattern specified on 27 January 1885 to replace the old red-and-white thirteen-stripe pattern with a blue field and yellow stars adopted in 1863.

Left: The gold lace strap with yellow center stripe for the music pouch, set out in specifications dated 5 April 1887, is evident here as are the shoulder knots with aiguillettes of cavalry trombonist John McCauley in his 1887-pattern musician's dress coat with dark yellow facings. (UK)

Below: Bandsmen of the Seventh Cavalry are less formal in their 1898- and 1899-pattern khaki blouses (the former having stand-up collar, the latter rolling collar) with yellow shoulder-tabs. The drum major, seated left of center, is wearing 1901-pattern chevrons with crossed buttons.

Above: Besides the 1895-pattern forage cap the Sixth Cavalry band at Fort Riley, Kansas had the canvas saddle cloth that began to replace saddle blankets by the 1890s. This image dates from 1900. (UK)

Right: Second Lieutenant Allen Keyes and his lady sat for their photograph in 1901, the same year that Keyes' officers' white blouse with shoulder loops and insignia was prescribed. He is wearing the gold crossed saber insignia of the Fourteenth Cavalry, on each side of the stand-up white mohair collar. The 1895-pattern officers' white cap was to be plain except for a yellow silk cord strap similar to the 1883-pattern gold version. The Arms of the United States appear on the loops of his straps which would also have a silver bar if he were a first lieutenant or a pair of silver bars at each end if he were a captain. Not until 1917 did second lieutenants receive rank insignia (a gold bar). (UK)

Right: Another young cavalry second lieutenant appears with the stand-up collar mohair blouse which was adopted in 1895 and which continued to be used into the twentieth century. The gilt eagles (Arms of the United States) are of the type prescribed in 1903 but replaced in 1904 by block style 'U.S' insignia. (USCM)

Left: First Lieutenant Henry Gibbons, Ninth Cavalry, is wearing the olive drab 1903-pattern service jacket with matching breeches, both in wool for winter wear. He too has the short-lived eagle insignia on his collar (discontinued in 1904) and the larger subdued eagle device on his olive drab cap with black visor and black chin strap. His watch fob with stirrup is non-regulation but adds to his appearance as a cavalry officer. (FAM)

Above: At the end of 1902 a major uniform change was promulgated which called for numerous new patterns, although a number of previously issued items remained in service as indicated by this private stationed at Fort Walla Walla, Washington, *circa* 1905. He is wearing the five-button blue woollen blouse, among other nineteenth-century vestiges, although he has the new Springfield .30 caliber bolt-action in his rifle scabbard, a weapon which began to replace the Krag from 1903. (CBFC)

Left: The regulation uniform called for at the end of 1902 included a full dress uniform for enlisted men consisting of a dark blue coat with six buttons. The shoulder loops, collar, and cuffs were trimmed in yellow mohair piping. A pair of yellow stripes of facing material were sewn on a detachable blue woollen band to be worn on the 'bellcrown' cap, while a worsted yellow breast cord formed another part of the gala or parade kit. (Herb Peck, Jr. Collection)

Left: By removing the hat band and breast cord, the full dress enlisted uniform prescribed at the end of 1902 by General Order No. 30 could be converted to the dress uniform for enlisted men. The collar and cap insignia remained the same as did the coat and sky-blue kersey trousers.

Below: The various uniform changes for enlisted men ushered in by General Order No. 130, 31 December 1902, are very evident in this photograph of Sixth Cavalry troopers. In the back row on the left is a soldier in the olive drab woollen overcoat with detachable hood. Next to him is a corporal in the cotton khaki service uniform and 1903-pattern campaign hat, while the private right of center and the one seated in the front row left are both wearing the dress uniform. The other seated figure is in the OD wool service dress, while the last figure in the muskrat cap, which was adopted in 1876, wears the medium brown canvas blanket-lined overcoat of the 1883-pattern with one-finger 1884-pattern mittens of canvas. This man's overshoes are of the 1889-pattern. The guidon seems to be a prop, being much larger than the three feet five inches by two feet three inches swallow tail prescribed on 27 January 1885. (CBFC)

Above: Bandsmen, such as these musicians from the Tenth Cavalry at Fort D. A. Russell, Wyoming, in 1911 or 1912, had the same uniform as the other ranks for dress and full dress, but exchanged a lyre for crossed sabers as their insignia. Additionally, they continued to display the double ½-inch stripes of yellow facing material on their trousers. Several of the men also bear service stripes on their coats. (Wyoming State Museum)

Right: Olive drab was introduced with the uniform adopted by General Orders No. 130, 30 December 1902. These two men from Troop 'M', Tenth Cavalry, are wearing the 1904-pattern flannel OD shirts with canvas olive drab breeches held up by russet leather belts. One of the men has modified his 1902-pattern campaign hat to give it a peak. In 1911 the next version of the campaign hat would be shaped in this fashion. Note also that canvas leggings replaced leather boots for cavalry enlisted men after several years of this type of footgear being phased out in favor of shoes and leggings. (KU)

Above: Wearing the dress uniform of the 1902-pattern, enlisted men and officers of the Eleventh Cavalry gather for a parade. This picture was taken in about 1913. (GH)

Left: In 1912 the full dress hat replaced the dress hat with mohair band, as seen here worn by Colonel James Parker, commander of the Eleventh Cavalry. His cap has gold embroidered 'scrambled eggs' on the black visor, an indication that he is a field grade officer. The band of the cap is yellow with gold bullion stripes on each side. Black mohair trims the 1902-pattern dress jacket with its concealed buttons. Service ribbons appear on the chest, having been introduced for that purpose in 1907. The breeches are light blue with 1½-inch leg stripes. (GH)

Right: Lieutenant Colonel Charles Young (the third African American graduate of West Point) wears olive drab shirt and breeches, both of wool, custom leather boots with combined laces and straps, and the 1911-pattern O.D. campaign hat with black and gold officers' cord, during military operations along the Mexican Border in 1915–16. (NA)

Left: The M1912 horse equipment was European-inspired. Innovative features included the method of slinging the 1903 Springfield rifle to the waist when mounted, with the butt of the stock resting in a bucket. While used on the Mexican-American Border during the 1916 Punitive Expedition, this experiment did not replace the McClellan saddle which had been in use since just before the Civil War and which remained pre-eminent until the demise of the U.S. Cavalry. The man is wearing the chevrons of a troop quartermaster sergeant on his 1910-pattern olive drab shirt, which could be worn in the field and for similar duties in lieu of the service coat, according to the 1912 *Uniform Regulations*. (RK)

Left: Members of Troop 'I', Sixth Cavalry, in France during the summer of 1918. The 'US' brand on a horse's shoulder is plain to see. The other partially visible horse on the left has an M1913 saber in its olive drab scabbard strapped to the rear left side of the saddle. (JSM)

Opposite page, bottom: The 1911-pattern olive drab service coat had a stand-up collar and had a circular device in lieu of the crossed saber insignia previously worn on uniform jackets. These bronze 'discs' had screwbacks and measured 1 inch in diameter. The disc on the left side of the collar was to bear crossed sabers with the regimental numeral above and the company letter below, when appropriate. The disc on the right side of the collar bore a 'U.S.'. As of 30 December 1916, these insignia could be worn on the shirt if the coat was not being worn as the outer garment. This trooper has slung the M1912 cavalry bandoleer across his shoulder to the hip and has the M1912 pistol holster. Again, the horse equipment is of the M1912 type. (RK)

Below: E. G. Hungerford, Troop 'I', Sixth Cavalry, wears the M1917 steel helmet with the 1911-pattern service coat and accouterments typical of American troops in France during the Great War. The horses in the background are fully loaded for the field. (JSM)

Left: George S. Patton appears in the 1902-pattern officers' full dress coat of a major, which was seldom used after the outbreak of the Great War. Patton, however, was fashion-conscious, and this handsome dark blue coat with contrasting light blue trousers bearing a 1½-inch yellow stripe down each outer seam was just the thing to show off his decorations earned during the years 1916 to 1918. He likewise holds the M1913 straight-blade saber which has been nicknamed after him in more recent times. (NA)

Below: This trooper standing to horse exemplifies the post-war cavalryman. He is wearing the 1910-pattern pullover shirt and breeches of olive drab, with an M1916 holster on an M1910 mounted cartridge belt, held by M1907 suspenders. His M1911 spurs, and the canvas leggings of which numerous models were made and issued are in evidence, although gauntlets are not, these accessories having essentially disappeared in lieu of riding gloves or bare hands. (KHC)

Above: The Tenth Cavalry regimental drum corps cut an imposing figure as seen in this 1921 picture in their olive drab service uniform of the period. (Fort Huachuca Museum)

Below: Typical of the mid to late 1930s field uniform, these troopers gallop at breakneck in 1911-pattern campaign hats, olive drab pullover shirts with matching breeches, M1931 boots, and riding gloves. (KHC)

Opposite page, top: Riding into history, the 1911-pattern campaign hats of these troopers near Marfa, Texas, in 1935, bear the distinctive regimental insignia, almost the only way of telling what outfit these men belonged to once they went into the field.

Below: A review of the First Cavalry Division in 1938 includes bandsmen. Most of the troops have the 1911-pattern campaign hat, although some appear in the field or garrison cap authorized for personnel of mechanized cavalry units. Both Oxford-style pullovers and the 'coat style' shirt, the latter being adopted in 1934, are evident. The shirts are olive drab, khaki versions not being issued until after June 1934. But khaki cotton breeches were issued, and are seen here as are M1931 boots, and three-buckle-type boots as well, although the latter were not officially sanctioned until 1940. Most officers here have the M1921 field belt, as well as the M1907 suspenders. (KHC)

Left: Both men and horses of this machine-gun troop put on gas masks for this charge during training exercises in Texas in about 1939. The uniforms and equipment are, for the most part, the same as those used during the Great War, with certain modifications. English-style skirts were added to the M1904 McClellan saddle in 1928. Lace-up boots replaced shoes and puttees in 1931. The holster lost its swivel after 1916. (KHC)

Below: Armored cars and scout cars joined tanks and horses in the post-war cavalry formations as represented here in the mid-1930s by this six-wheeled vehicle of Troop 'A', First Cavalry, the unit being designated by the traditional crossed sabers on the door and by a stylized version of the distinctive regimental insignia consisting of a black hawk on a gold eight-pointed star, to recall the old First Regiment of Dragoons' cap plate from 1833. (NA)

Left: A cavalry lieutenant colonel stands in front of a First Cavalry scout car in a private purchase 'coat style' shirt and undress riding boots. The circular patch on the field cap denotes branch of service, in this case yellow for cavalry. (KHC)

Left: A pre-Second World War armored vehicle, the M2 tank, bears markings which hark back to the days of the horse soldier, a red-and-white 1885-pattern guidon, in paint on metal rather than silk, being carried on a staff by a trooper. (KHC)

Above: The M2A1 scout car crossing a pontoon bridge during maneuvers in 1940 shows the future of the cavalry, which would give way to armor, and even to helicopters in later generations. (NA)

Right: One of the last mounted troopers gazes into an uncertain future. Still wearing a modified version of the steel pot adopted in the Great War, the most innovative item of clothing seen is the coat-type shirt which superseded the pullover shirt by the late 1930s. The laces of his 1931-pattern boots were replaced in 1940 by three buckles. The saddle is the 1928 modification of the M1904 McClellan. (KHC)

private on the right, William Cox, is wearing the 1911-pattern campaign hat and leather garrison belt. (KHC)

Above: A close-up of Private Cox shows the insignia on his lapels to be two 'U.S.' discs instead of one 'U.S.' and one with crossed sabers, because the trooper has not yet completed the cavalry school. The campaign hat is the 'beaver brown' felt instead of the drab color of the earlier version of this hat. The black mohair necktie lasted until 1942 when it was replaced by an olive drab version. (KHC)

Above: Two cavalry trainees stand before the door of their barracks at Camp Funston, Kansas, in November 1941. Both are wearing the 1939-pattern service coat with service breeches and 1940-pattern cavalry boots. The private on the left wears the olive drab garrison cap (overseas cap), the

Below: Despite the heat, a cavalry regimental band at Fort Bliss, Texas, appear in sleeves rolled down to the wrists, regulation style. Pistol belts are worn by the musicians, but for no evident purpose. (KHC)

Right: A cavalryman engages in one of the less glamorous aspects of horsemanship, wearing the denim work trousers and jacket adopted in 1940 to replace the previous pullover-type jacket first issued in 1908 to coast artillery troops, then extended for use by other branches. The trooper is also wearing the winter cap. (KHC)

Below: As the Second World War drew near for the United States, a two-piece herringbone twill work suit in green was adopted. This tanker standing on a M3 Grant tank is wearing the first pattern. (NA)

Above: In this picture taken in May 1941, cavalrymen, trading horses for tanks and other vehicles, are wearing the newly adopted khaki shirt, although the tankers at Fort Knox, Kentucky, are still wearing the 1931-pattern mounted boots, together with the composite tanker helmet and goggles.

Right: Motorcycles, jeeps, scout cars, and half-tracks have replaced steady steeds as this mechanized cavalry column motors along a river bed on maneuvers not long before Pearl Harbor thrust the United States into the Second World War. (NA)

Right: Members of the Constabulary formed for duty in Germany from 1946 to 1952 wear the M1A1 helmet liner, the 1944-pattern olive drab field European Theater of Operations field jacket, popularly known as the 'Ike' jacket, olive drab trousers, and olive drab shirt with khaki tie. The sergeant on the left was a member of the 8th Armored Division during the Second World War as indicated by his triangular shoulder sleeve insignia. The man leading the horse has distinctive unit insignia on the lower lapels of his jacket to indicate that he is a member of the Fourth Constabulary Regiment. He is wearing the ribbons of his Good Conduct Medal and Occupation of Germany Service Medal, the former being nearest the center of the jacket. (SSE)

Right: The shoulder sleeve insignia with yellow centers and a 'C' with a lightning bolt together with the tab above designated Constabulary troops, as seen here during an inspection by a major of two NCOs of this unit. Once again, the men are from the Fourth Constabulary Regiment, formerly the Fourth Cavalry. Their three-buckle boots, and the fact that the corporal on the right has placed the holster for his .45 caliber semi-automatic pistol cross-draw style on his left hip suspended from a white web belt, are indications of the cavalry lineage of this unit. (SSE)